Davia M. Woodward

ELOHAI
INTERNATIONAL

Published by ELOHAI International Publishing & Media:
P.O. Box 64402
Virginia Beach, VA 23467
Elohaipublishing.com

ISBN: 978-1-7348778-8-5

Dedication

This book is dedicated to all the kids who had challenges or hard times growing up.

Acknowledgements

I want to acknowledge my mom Sharita Woodward for helping to push me to write this book even when I felt like I didn't want do anymore. I also want to thank my aunt Ni for helping me to push forward and for telling me, "You got this. When the end results come out you're going to be happy and joyful to know that you wrote your book by yourself." I also want to thank my grandfather, Thornell McLauchlin.for sitting me down and having the time to listen to what I was saying and doing when I was writing my book, for listening to what I was going through, and helping me throughout the whole process.

Table of Contents

Introducing me

Hello my name is Davia, and I am a thirteen-year-old girl and my birthday is September 8, 2006. I enjoy cheerleading, singing, dancing, baking, and making money. I am an honor roll student and have been since I started school. I am also currently taking AP classes while only in the 7th grade. Amazing right? For all of my hard work in my honors classes, I was awarded a Certificate of Outstanding Academic Excellence from Kappa Alpha Psi Fraternity, Inc. When I get older, I plan on owning my own nail salon. I'm happy in life right now, but it hasn't always been this way.

My life has been a rollercoaster ride as far as my dad is concerned. I say that because it's been good and bad, and I often really don't know what I'll get. My dad is a good person when he wants to be, however, he lets anger and immaturity run his life. This, in turn, has affected me in ways that I'm learning to understand, but not accept and change me for the worst. Honestly, if I could be real with my dad, I would tell him to grow up and show up! I'm really not sure how many kids my dad has. I'll say six to be on the safe side. It makes me sad that I'm not close with my siblings. We don't talk, we don't even know each other, and that is all because of my dad's lifestyle.

My mom told me to write my feelings out to help in a healing process, so here it is. It has helped me so much that I wanted to share my story to help other children who may be going through an absent parent situation and who may feel alone. Remember you are not alone. God will always be there!

I thought about it and my vision of a good dad is one that takes care of you. He's there for you when you need him the most. A good dad is one who will come to your birthday celebration, come to your games or competitions, and cheer you on through life. He will also accept you for who you are no matter if you're skinny, curvy, tall, or short. It all comes down to loving your son or daughter for who they are.

Growing up without a dad can be really hard. Seeing everyone with their dad and not having yours around sucks. Trust me I know. It makes you wonder "where's my dad," or "what happened to him?" You also ask yourself, "Does he even love me?" Don't worry though, it's not you. Remember he is missing out on an amazing son or daughter(s) at home. His bad decision is not a reflection of who you are.

When I was a baby, my mom and dad took care of me, then things went south. By the time I turned five, he let his attitude get the best of him, and his actions caused him to go to jail. He went to jail for three whole years, and get this, he said that he was not going to go back in there ever again. He said he was going to stop with all those bad habits he had. Fast forward, he went back to jail, then back to jail, then back again. So as you can tell, he has not been in my life at all because of his selfish ways and childish ways.

You're probably wondering how I feel about this whole thing. Well I feel angry at times because he always says he is going to come pick me up and never does. I used to cry and get mad at my mom. She said to stop calling him and leave him alone, but the only reason she said that was because of what my dad did the last time I called him. He disrespected me and called me all names besides my own. He stated that people are putting bad things in my head about him and other nonsense. By that time, though, I already knew how he was from his own actions. My mother never talked bad about him. She actually tried to make him seem better than what he was. I realized that my mom has been there for me and I thank her. She listens to me, and she doesn't just say she is listening. She really does, and she takes me seriously. So if your dad isn't around or vice versa and your mom is taking care of you and making sure you have what you need, appreciate her. Or if you have someone else that's taking care of you, appreciate them, they don't have to do it. I know you may want your dad around, but don't treat your mom mean and feel bad about life. You should feel happy because God said, "For my father and my mother forsake me, but the Lord myself shall take you in" (Psalm 27:10). Always remember that. It's what helps me.

There are times you may also want to cry. Just tell your mom, or, if you don't feel comfortable telling her, write it down. Don't keep it bottled up. You'll eventually explode and most times on the wrong person. I know you're tired of hearing that, but it's the truth. I had to learn it. It's not a good feeling... trust me on this one. God has blessed me a lot. He has sent people to help me with school, clothes, school supplies, and so much more. My uncles, mom, grandparents, aunts, and my mom's boyfriend helped me through the process of not having a father. They give me shoes and money to get my nails done, and they also give me great advice and words of encouragement. They cheer me on and they are there for me if I ever need them. Think of a positive person in your life that cares about you, and hug them and show them you care. It'll help you and them. Here is some advice: don't worry about your dad just move on forward with your life.I know it hurts that he isn't there but don't focus your attention on him because in the long run you will be glad you didn't. Focus on the people around you that are positive and will help you become better.

I wrote this book for children without a dad or mom and who may have the same problems I do. I want to help them with their emotions. If this is you, I want you to know how to handle the situation and not feel bad about your dad or mom not being around. I also wrote this book for me so that I may heal as well. Just live your life the best way you possibly can because you only get one life.

You are not any less than because of who decided to leave your life. You are still more than able to over achieve and be great. It's all about how you turn out because ultimately YOU still have a life to live. Remember to not become a victim and fall short in life. Things will always happen that may make you feel like giving up, but giving up is never the option. Everyday you wake up there is another opportunity to be great. Learn from the unfortunate things that may happen in your life and grow through them. Rise above it all like I have. Against the odds, I still conquer. You can and will too! Always remember YOU ARE MORE THAN ENOUGH!!!! Don't let bad thoughts live in your mind. Think yourself great and you will be great!

Now, make a book of your own with these next few pages. Read the quotes and scriptures on the next few pages, and afterwards, write down how they make you feel.

But those who hope in the Lord will renew their strength. They will soar on wings like eagles; they will walk and not be faint.

- Isaiah 40:31

When you pass through the waters, I will be with you; and when you pass through the rivers, they will not sweep over you. When you walk through fire, you will not be burned; the flames will not set you ablaze.

- Isaiah 43:2

Trust in the Lord with all your heart, And lean not on your own understanding; In all your ways acknowledge Him, And He shall direct your paths.

- Proverbs 3:5-6

So do not fear, for I am with you; do not be dismayed, for I am your God. I will strengthen you and help you; I will uphold you with my righteous right hand.

- Isaiah 41:10

“Dad always said to not allow people to stay in your life, and he was right because he was the first to leave.”

"It doesn't matter who you are, where you come from. The ability to triumph begins with you. Always."

– Oprah Winfrey

It doesn't matter how slowly you go as long as you don't stop."

– Confucius

"Anything's possible if you've got enough nerve."

– J.K. Rowling

About the Author

Davia Morgan is an eighth grader, who lives in Maryland. She enjoys spending time with her family, watching movies, playing in the pool, and going to cookouts. Davia participates in creative arts in school, and she also enjoys cooking, writing, science projects, and taking pictures. She is a member of the Girls with Pearls program, where she serves her community with other young women. Davia is an entrepreneur and she started her first business, Cakes by Davia, when she was in the third grade. In 2019, she launched Nails by Davia where she does acrylic manicures. Davia would like to become a photographer when she grows up. Follow her on Instagram @DaviaWoodward_1.

Connect and Share!

If you liked this book, and you feel other children and teens can benefit from it, please consider purchasing copies as gifts, leaving a review on Amazon.com, and sharing this book cover and title on your social media pages.

Follow @DaviaWoodward_1 on Instagram.

www.ingramcontent.com/pod-product-compliance
Lightning Source LLC
LaVergne TN
LVHW010548100826
845148LV00013B/2659

* 9 7 8 1 7 3 4 8 7 7 8 8 5 *